ALL
THE WAYS I'M A
NOMAD

ISBN: 154820224X
ISBN-13: 978-1548202248

www.atwian.com

For

my mother

whose strength knows

no bounds

To find the words

On you

Why
with you came poetry
like a flower grows from between
a rock and
a hard place.

It's that time of night
where I retire to my bed with
your memory by my side
and another day behind me
(*from the silence*)
the concertmaster strings out
his first notes
and as my nose plays out your scent
my lips play out your words
and my mind
slips away
to Neverland.

There is a voice in your eyes
that commands light
in corners of me
I never knew
were sitting in the dark.

When the summer's sunset
stirs your skin
and your shirt traces your back
like I used to
while the Tarmac sighs its last heat
and your bleary eyes glint off windows
of softened houses
as your breath settles on your chest
and the sky sets on fire
I hope you find me in the pink and yellow hues
there's something more forgiving
about summer afternoons.

You're stirring
galaxies
behind your
eyes and I love
nothing more
than to be a
stargazer
quietly
tracing the constellations
lighting up my
nights.

There are parts of me
yearning for parts of you
I have not met yet
this is how
love is blind.

I could listen
to the way you
think for hours.

Call me superficial
but I have never envied material things
any less than wine
envies the glass
that meets his lips
wool
the scarf that drapes around his neck
and linen
the covers on his pillows
to hear
the breaths
that pass.

You're the sweeping wind
to the wildfire of my mind
this is why
I flicker at your name.

The question is not
whether you were loved
it's whether you were loved
enough.

-   *know the difference*

I will always
remember you
the night time star
from the winter of my life
and how I will *remember*
how you left me
out in the cold
alone.

  -   *misled*

Simultaneously
losing
and finding yourself
in someone else.

- *the idea of love*

The type of boy
to leave a glacier like me
a dripping puddle in his hands
a blizzard so frantic
it wouldn't know
it was settling into
crisp
new
beginnings.

Growing up
I did not know love
was so close to me
but as it turns out
love was just
a glance
away.

How is it
that even when the
only colours I've left
on my palette are gritted
greys and solemn blues
you still seem to paint
such a wonderful
picture?

You smell like the sweetest
last chance I grant my vices
and the first time I forgot
that I was trying to
forget you.

Please don't punish me
for missing you
do you know
what torture it is
for me to see you
in everything
but my life?

I find people die quicker
when you let your mind
run far and wide
with who you believe they
could be
rather than who they are
which seems like a good idea until
they fall down the gap between
becoming somebody you want
rather than the person you need
to learn from.

- *expectation*

You are such a full moon
a distance between horizon and sky
so far apart
the heart doesn't grow fonder
it grows *weaker*
'cause you keep pulling me back
to my knees every night
until the morning chases you away
until 2:37 a.m. the next day
where I'll fall to my knees again
to the shores where I sit
and listen to the waves
slowly crashing
to the beat of an ocean
that is my heart.

If actions
speak louder
than words
your silence is
deafening.

I intend on using you
as leverage
by taking everything
you took from me
I will use loss
for gain
and make a medal
out of the battle
within me
over you.

I never
knew I
could choke
on words the
way your
tongue
has
knotted my
throat.

It's not so much
that my heart stopped
beating but more that
like the waves plead
the shore at night
it crashes
a little softer
sighs
a little longer
now
that I listen
alone.

I'm trying to untie
myself from your name
but all it's leaving is
loose ends.

I should've sailed
around the world by now and
I guess in many ways I have
but I think I erred in thinking
you were the harbour
and not the ocean.

It is a most sorry
recipe
to have two people
quite whole apart
but never quite whole
together
suffering that they cannot have
each other in bits
and can't not have each other
at all.

I guess I can explain the lack of us
through poetic differences;
you wrote about her
and I still write about you.

I could never have dreamt you
into existence
and now here I am
losing sleep 'cause
I can't seem to dream you
out of it.

All my feelings
have known you
and I don't know
how to feel
about that.

It's hard not to
believe in miracles
when I've mourned you
a hundred times.

You must learn
not to want that thing
that does not
want you.

If this is failed
infatuation
I don't want to know true heartbreak
I'm not sure I could ever know
such an avalanche
and live to tell the tale.

(yet here we are)

If loving yourself *more*
means loving them *less*
that boy
is not
the one.

Sometimes we fear
walking away from the people we love
not because they might betray us
but because they simply might not follow
and surely that feels
like the biggest betrayal of all.

- *and what if we stayed?*

You have no place
in the dreams of someone
who does not dare
to believe.

Do not lose yourself
trying not to lose
somebody else.

I swallowed my pride for you
so it hurts to see
you find it
so easy
to chew me up
and spit me back out
as if the sweet nothings you fed me
had soured in your mouth
instead of mine.

I don't miss you
I am *missing* you
you have opened up parts of me
and left them aching for company.

Do not
waste my time
then come to me one day
telling me I was right
that *we* were right
do not be that person
that I was
pushing people away
because I wrote poems that said

If I ever make you feel
unwanted
I'm sorry
it's just
I don't like to see people
go
and I can't believe
you would
stay.

All the poetry in the world
and not a stanza
sentence
or letter
to rewrite such
an ending.

Longing has brought me
the time to learn
not to let it go
but to let it *be*.

Life is becoming
sweeter
than the thought of
you.

I guess you'll just have to
spend the rest of your life
without me
a savoured memory
in a book of all
my favourite
poetry.

So what
she speaks in flowers
I speak in
earth
and water
and you said yourself
I am fire
so
I'm sure you can understand
I cannot offer the *world*
to someone who seeks only to be an island
never venturing a stone's throw further
than the moats he has built
around his
heart.

Would love be
as love is
if love was something
we could help
but do?

No good reason
to stay
is good enough reason
to go.

It is better to miss
somebody else
than to be with that person
spending your days
missing yourself.

Look at all the flowers
I've grown from you.

I am blessed
to have lost
and gained enough
to know
it does not matter
if it hurts today
nothing is forever
so as I came
so I will go
and in the end
I will be just fine
without you.

Be sure not to mistake the rush
of clutching wilting roses
in your palms for the
stretching and yearning that
erupted in spring
you won't be able to stem
the flow from the cuts
you've outgrown this Eden
walk out
Adam lost
this Eve.

Good mourning
dear

- new day

On me

Sometimes we are great mountains
and sometimes we are thundering avalanches
it is how we rise and fall from grace
that makes us beautiful.

Gizem Erdoğan

There are black holes
sinking in my chest
and yet
I'm not sure who needs
the other to survive
more.

- *look after your mind*

I am not cold
I am *exhausted*
from using my light
to keep others warm
even though I know
they have no intention
of keeping their fire going
'cause they seem to think
I will never tire
from putting out
my own.

There's this thing
carving out my insides
making less room for me
and more room for nothing
a sort of hollowed heaviness
where in the middle I sit
a hostage to this thing
trying to figure out
what it is
my body is grieving.

I'm sorry
that you are a puddle of
sadness
that you are drowning
from the inside out.

I thought
perhaps
if I wrote enough
I'd be immortalized
so my mistakes could be left
to having all the time in the world
to know better
than wasting my time and feelings
waiting on people
who never waited
on leaving me.

If we are made
almost entirely of unfinished
business is it any wonder we
sometimes fall
apart?

I know I should
stick to more
traditional
therapies
but when has plucking at my heart-
strings ever produced anything
less than
symphony?

I think the reason
I cannot accept love
is because I can't tell
if it's right to find your love
tied up in
someone else
before you've found it
in yourself.

Survival
is being left in the wild and
making peace
with the creatures that lurk
within you.

I want to be loved
the way I want to love myself;
relentlessly.

Stop discrediting yourself
strength
with no other option
is still strength.

-   *as if surviving isn't enough*

You have felt emotions
in such extremes
is it not a testament to
how wonderful
your mind is?

I have ran out of places
to put my problems
sometimes they spill in tears
and sometimes they spill
in ink.

The idea
of being
broken
yet
whole.

If you hurt me
and I lose my kindness
have I not lost twice
and more?

Finding home in yourself
is the only embrace
that will set you free.

Do not confuse
your nurture
for your nature.

- *you are not your circumstances*

You cannot change
how you were raised
instead you can change
how you raise yourself.

- *there are mothers in all of us*

Working on myself
for myself
by myself
but most importantly
with myself.

But
I'm not sure when I stopped
writing for myself
and started writing for you.

-    *to the reader*

I am that fine line
between love and hate
and it is taking both parts of me
to learn
to stop taking sides
against myself.

Time heals all
at least
a little.

Know the hands
that deserve
to hold you.

We do not stop believing
in the sun
because it is a cloudy day
much less
we do not stop believing
it will rise again
tomorrow.

-    *and what of your life?*

Only ever
growing
in places of
quiet.

I lose faith in my work
everyday
now imagine
if I had let that stop me.

I know why
the caged
heart sings.

(homage to Maya Angelou)

Before you start
looking for something
anything
take a moment to remind yourself
you may not yet know
what it looks like.

I hope
you can
smell me
on my poems.

(they used to reek of you)

I always keep good company;
between my ribs
in my wrists
etched into my palms

good company starts in myself.

- *who else?*

The more
we savour
the less
we need.

Love yourself
for better
for worse
forever.

Thunder speaks to me
more than the sun
a war between the
elements
a rare violence
deep in the art
of beauty
even in disaster.

Seek to master
that which
frightens you
most.

What part of you
carrying this much
on your heart
makes you weak?

I am urging you
if you are reading this and
in your heart
you know something is up
that thing you're ignoring
that no one will understand
that you don't understand
that there is no help for
first for yourself
please
speak to someone about it.

- *please*

The same thing that
ties me to life is
my undoing.

Nothing is forever
cherish this for both its meanings.

(this is how you love life)

I
sometimes
turn wine back
into salt
water.

(and you say I keep unholy habits)

It is hard
to live your life in
constant belief that
despite it all
someone else could've lived it
better than you.

- *self-sabotage*

Do not orphan your flaws
(as you call them)
without them you are only half
a rose.

Fear is
the stories we tell
ourselves about the
dark but I think those
stories say a lot more
about us than they do
the dark.

I am letting things go
to free up my heart
for other things
so make no mistake
when I forgive
I forgive for me
and not for you.

Sometimes your mind is
a chaos and poems like this
are the only way
to straighten
it out.

The thing with silver linings is that
they either gilt your armour
or cut you clean in half.

(but always leave you brighter)

Learning to love yourself
might just be
the bravest thing
you will ever do in your life.

My roots are buried in two different
countries that I call my *home*
in two different
languages that I call my *tongue*
perhaps this is why I'm always so torn
between who I am
and who I am meant to be.

-   *British Asian (Other)*

Writing is so much easier
if you take every word you utter
every thought that crosses your path
as art
you are art.

I'm falling in love with life
for the first time
all over again.

(it gets better)

So many parts of you have died
for you to be living as you are now
do not confuse loss
for death
when the world has ended for you
so many times before.

Make friends
with life
you owe each other nothing
start there.

I've only just
grown
young.

On people

I tried to
find myself
in other people
instead
I found myself
picking up pieces
of shrapnel
lacing London's
concrete pavements
trying to collect myself
into already broken arms.

You reap what you sow;
quit making cemeteries
out of people.

Do not tell me
I need your affections
I loved myself before you did
just as I hated myself before you do.

- *entitlement*

It is the
workings of a
misinformed
parent
to leave their
daughter to remind
them

my body is always
and only
mine

and so
yes
believe me
I'd be disappointed
if I had a child like
you too.

Be the lesson
not the collateral
damage.

Family
that is toxic
is still
toxic.

No sound more
grotesque
than that of a man
chewing up
and spitting out the worlds
he promised his wife
then asking her why she's
not an appetite for him.

- *your breath reeks*

I need a strong man
yes
a man so strong
when I open myself up to him like this
he reaches for the strength in his heart
and not in his wrists
to be able to carry all of me
and bear the weight of my words
without shutting the book in fear
when I say
I need a strong man
yes
I need a man who feels
more than he hides
who thinks
more than he speaks
and who fears no thing
but a fear of feeling itself.

She seeks you in every
man she meets
in every hand
she holds but if
she is searching
is she really even searching
for you?

-     *to be a father*

If he keeps trying to break
you then make love to
you what does that tell you
other than
the only broken plaything that
was missing from his
childhood was
a glass ceiling and that
perhaps it's high time someone
taught that boy
that you don't throw rocks in
glasshouses and get away
with not having to play
in the shards.

She has roses blooming
in her eyes for a man
that has never seen
spring.

A true test of wealth
came in the form of
me deserving an apology
and you not being able
to afford me even
that.

You know
you've made yourself
a very interesting habit
of bending over backwards
to stab yourself in the back
to be paid attention by people
who would have done it for you
for free.

The things they don't have
the courage
to say to your face
they will have you feel
in your heart
instead.

If you are made to feel
temporary
let them taste the loss of you
allow yourself to slip through
their fingers
and one day they will look for you
and all they will see
will be the hands that weren't
big enough
to hold you.

Sometimes
you cannot see the
light at the end of the tunnel
because you're allowing
certain people
to stand in your way.

Distance yourself
from the people and things
that distance you
from you.

Integrity
is refusing to be
complicit
in your own
fetishisation.

Stop
romanticizing
mental
health.

That is all.

Walking into people
and walking out
a different person.

Istanbul
I miss you
and even that
is something to be
cherished.

Small cities
are for people
who have already
found themselves.

These poems have no meaning
without people like you
people with hearts
that have known pain
to bring them to life
they are warm
because you have the same fire
within you.

All of us
coming together
trickling down in
streams
growing into rivers
spilling over into
oceans
bringing our pain together
in our descent
using the very thing
that broke us apart to
mend us better
and that is so
so precious to me.

- *antivenom*

My mother's strength
leaves me in awe
and fear
at the same time.

You tell me you read people
that you see me going far
going places
that's so kind
thank you
I'm hoping to reference
what you said later
maybe in a
memoir
maybe in a
dark room
where I'll need those lovely
rosy glasses to see
what masterpiece you saw in a
scribble like me
and then I guess I'll
thank you again
for reminding me that art
is in the eye of the person who
sees beauty
even in
disaster.

You make me question
everything good
I've ever nurtured about myself
'cause you're the kind of soul
that would've been born beautiful
any way nature intended.

And if you are stirred up
by seeing your soul
stretched through the pages of a
book
written by a girl
you've never met from a
country you've never set foot on then
don't you think it's time you let yourself
have the honour of accepting your
struggles and pains are deserving of awards
and your mind is as beautiful as your soul
just as people have been telling you since
you could even think
that you were anything less than
whole.

Thank you.

Gizem Erdoğan

Acknowledgements

Special thanks to my illustrator Mariam Marzouk for her wonderful work and patience in working with me.

Many thanks also to Jean Anne Heng for my cover art, it's beautiful and has become even more symbolic than I could've ever imagined.

I also want to thank anyone who showed me support and kindness when I had nothing to offer them in return, you have truly inspired me and thus, this work.

Thank you.

Gizem Erdoğan

About the author

Gizem Erdoğan is a Turkish poet and writer, born and raised in Newcastle-Upon-Tyne, UK. From a young age, she's been a creative with a passion for horse-riding and drawing. Though her drawing took more of a backseat over the years, horses remained one of her greatest passions. Gizem started writing regularly in 2014 after deciding to re-explore poetry and creative writing as something she had especially enjoyed at school as a way of being able to express herself. Soon after she began writing pieces—or sometimes, pieces of pieces—as they came to her in the notes on her phone, she had accumulated a small portfolio of prose - little thoughts and reflections she encountered and made as she went about pursuing a career in Finance as an Economics student in London. After performing some of her pieces at The Poetry Place in Holborn, she would occasionally drop poems on her Instagram as a way of dipping her toe into the water. After a few months, some positive feedback and an increasing flow of prose, she felt it was time to give her work more identity and in September 2016 created @nomadic_words on Instagram, with the hope of one day publishing a book of her work, bringing us to where we are today.

61395592R00082

Made in the USA
San Bernardino, CA
14 December 2017